The Acts of Saint Andrew

By Andrew

Copyright © 2022 Lamp of Trismegistus. All rights reserved. No part of this publication may be reproduced or transmitted in any form or by any means, electronic or mechanical, including photocopying, recording, or by any information storage and retrieval system, without permission in writing from Lamp of Trismegistus. Reviewers may quote brief passages.

ISBN: 978-1-63118-623-3

Christian Apocrypha Series

Other Books in this Series and Related Titles

The Acts of the Apostle John by John (978-1-63118-622-6)

The Ascension of Isaiah by Isaiah (978-1-63118-620-2)

The Book of Wisdom of Solomon by King Solomon (978-1-63118-502-1)

The Apocalypse of Peter by Peter (978-1-63118-527-4)

The Gospel of the Nativity of Mary by St. Matthew (978-1-63118-448-2)

The Vision of Saint Paul the Apostle by Paul (978-1-63118-526-7)

Early Translation of the Acts of the Apostles by Luke (978-1-63118-521-2)

The Hymn of Jesus by G. R. S. Mead (978-1-63118-409-3)

Psalms of Solomon by King Solomon (978-1-63118-439-0)

The First and Second Gospels of the Infancy of Jesus Christ (978-1-63118-415-4)

The Book of Parables by Enoch (978-1-63118-429-1)

The Testament of Abraham by Abraham (978-1-63118-441-3)

The Lives of Adam and Eve by Moses (978-1-63118-414-7)

Fourth Book of Maccabees by Josephus (978-1-63118-562-5)

Book of the Watchers by Enoch (978-1-63118-615-8)

Lost Chapters of the Book of Daniel and Related Writings (978-1-63118-417-8)

The Testament of Moses by Moses (978-1-63118-440-6)

Testaments of the Twelve Patriarchs (978-1-63118-579-3)

The Story of Ahikar by Ahiqar (978-1-63118-561-8)

The Odes of Solomon by King Solomon (978-1-63118-503-8)

The Book of Astronomical Secrets by Enoch (978-1-63118-443-7)

Audio Versions are also Available on Audible, Amazon and Apple

Other Books in this Series and Related Titles

The Hidden Mysteries of Christianity by Annie Besant (978–1–63118–534–2)

Second Book of Enoch by Enoch (978-1-63118-617-2)

The Hymns of Hermes by G. R. S. Mead (978-1-63118-405-5)

Freemasonry and the Egyptian Mysteries by C. W. Leadbeater (978-1-63118-456-7)

The Sepher Yetzirah and the Qabalah by M P Hall (978-1-63118-481-9)

Book of Dreams by Enoch (978-1-63118-437-6)

The Historic, Mythic and Mystic Christ by Annie Besant (978–1–63118–533–5)

The Fourth-Gospel and Synoptical Problem by G R S Mead (978–1–63118–576–2)

Masonic Symbolism of King Solomon's Temple by A Mackey &c (978-1-63118-442-0)

The Crest-Jewel of Wisdom by Adi Shankara (978-1-63118-475-8)

Kali the Mother by Sister Nivedita (978-1-63118-558-8)

The Brotherhood of Religions by Annie Besant (978–1–63118–563–2)

What Theosophy Does for Us by C W Leadbeater (978–1–63118–574–8)

Buddhist Psalms by Shinran (978-1-63118-465-9)

Catholicism, Yoga and Hinduism by Hartmann &c (978-1-63118-478-9)

Masonic Symbolism of Easter and the Christ in Masonry (978-1-63118-434-5)

Tao Te Ching & Commentary by Lao Tzu & C Johnston (978-1-63118-495-6)

Ancient Mysteries and Secret Societies by M P Hall (978-1-63118-410-9)

The Golden Verses of Pythagoras: Five Translations (978-1-63118-479-6)

Freemasonry & Catholicism by Max Heindel (978-1-63118-508-3)

A Few Masonic Sermons by A. C. Ward &c (978-1-63118-435-2)

Audio versions are also available on Audible, Amazon and Apple

Table of Contents

Series Introduction...7

The Acts of Saint Andrew

Introduction...9

Primary Translation...11

Fragments...26

The Martyrdom...36

Secondary Translation...45

SERIES INTRODUCTION

The Apocrypha are a loosely knit series of books, written by early vanguards of Christianity (covering the eras of both the old and new testaments), and which comprise somewhere between about a dozen to several hundred titles, depending on whom you ask and how that person defines "Apocrypha." A small selection of these can still be found included in the Catholic bible, while a majority of the books in question, were abandoned by church officials in the early centuries of Christianity. Many of these apocryphal books were originally considered canon by early followers of Christ, in the first four centuries following his birth. It wasn't until the meeting of the Council of Nicaea in 325, that Emperor Constantine and a group of roughly 300 church bishops, gathered together with the goal of defining, standardizing and unifying an otherwise splintering Christianity, that many of these writings ceased to be included in the newly established canon. Enjoy then, this book as an example, of just one of the many books of the Christian Apocrypha, and be sure to check out other titles in this series.

Introduction

We have no ancient record of the length of this book, as we had in the cases of John, Paul, and Peter (but I suspect it was the most prolix of all the five), and we have fewer relics of the original text than for those. We have, however, a kind of abstract of the whole, written in Latin by Gregory of Tours: and there are Greek Encomia of the apostle which also help to the reconstruction of the story. The Martyrdom (as in other cases) exists separately, in many texts. Max Bonnet has established the relations of these to each other: and J. Flamion has made a most careful study of all the fragments.

The best specimen of the original text which we have is a fragment preserved in a Vatican MS., tenth-eleventh centuries, containing discourses of Andrew shortly before his passion. There are also a few ancient quotations.

These Acts may be the latest of the five leading apostolic romances. They belong to the third century: C. A. D. 260?

It was formerly thought that the Acts of Andrew and Matthias (Matthew) were an episode of the original romance: but this view has ceased to be held. That legend is akin to the later Egyptian romances about the apostles of which an immense number were produced in the fifth and later centuries. An abstract of them will be given in due course.

The epitome by Gregory of Tours is considered by Flamion to give on the whole the best idea of the contents of the original Acts. The latest edition of it is that by M. Bonnet in the Monumenta Germaniac Historica (Greg. Turon. II. 821-47). The greater part appears as Lib. III of the Historia Apostolica of (Pseudo-)Abdias, in a text much altered, it seems, in the sixteenth century by Wolfgang Lazius: reprinted in Fabricius' Cod. Apocr. N. T.

Gregory's prologue is as follows:

The famous triumphs of the apostles are, I believe, not unknown to any of the faithful, for some of them are taught us in the pages of the gospel, others are related in the Acts of the Apostles, and about some of them books exist in which the actions of each apostle are recorded; yet of the more part we have nothing but their Passions in writing.

Now I have come upon a book on the miracles (virtues, great deeds) of St. Andrew the apostle, which, because of its excessive verbosity, was called by some apocryphal. And of this I thought good to extract and set out the 'virtues' only, omitting all that bred weariness, and so include the wonderful miracles within the compass of one small volume, which might both please the reader and ward off the spite of the adverse critic: for it is not the multitude of words, but the soundness of reason and the purity of mind that produce unblemished faith.

The Acts of Saint Andrew
Primary Translation

1 After the Ascension the apostles dispersed to preach in various countries. Andrew began in the province of Achaia, but Matthew went to the city of Mermidona.

2 Andrew left Mermidona and came back to his own allotted district. Walking with his disciples he met a blind man who said: 'Andrew, apostle of Christ, I know you can restore my sight, but I do not wish for that: only bid those with you to give me enough money to clothe and feed myself decently.' Andrew said: 'This is the devil's voice, who will not allow the man to recover his sight.' He touched his eyes and healed him. Then, as be had but a vile rough garment, Andrew said: 'Take the filthy garment off him and clothe him afresh.' All were ready to strip themselves, and Andrew said: 'Let him have what will suffice him.' He returned home thankful.

3 Demetrius of Amasea had an Egyptian boy of whom he was very fond, who died of a fever. Demetrius hearing of Andrew's miracles, came, fell at his feet, and besought help. Andrew pitied him, came to the house, held a very long discourse, turned to the bier, raised the boy, and restored him to his master. All believed and were baptized.

4 A Christian lad named Sostratus came to Andrew privately and told him: 'My mother cherishes a guilty passion for me: I have repulsed her, and she has gone to the proconsul to throw the guilt on me. I would rather die than expose her.' The officers came to fetch the boy, and Andrew prayed and went with him. The mother accused him. The proconsul bade him defend himself. He was silent, and so continued, until the proconsul retired to take counsel. The mother began to weep. Andrew said: 'Unhappy woman, that dost not fear to cast thine own guilt on thy son.' She said to the proconsul: 'Ever since my son entertained his wicked wish he has been in constant company with this man.' The proconsul was enraged, ordered the lad to be sewn into the leather bag of parricides and drowned in the river, and Andrew to be imprisoned till his punishment

should be devised. Andrew prayed, there was an earthquake, the proconsul fell from his seat, everyone was prostrated, and the mother withered up and died. The proconsul fell at Andrew's feet praying for mercy. The earthquake and thunder ceased, and he healed those who had been hurt. The proconsul and his house were baptized.

5 The son of Cratinus (Gratinus) of Sinope bathed in the women's bath and was seized by a demon. Cratinus wrote to Andrew for help: he himself had a fever and his wife dropsy. Andrew went there in a vehicle. The boy tormented by the evil spirit fell at his feet. He bade it depart and so it did, with outcries. He then went to Cratinus' bed and told him he well deserved to suffer because of his loose life, and bade him rise and sin no more. He was healed. The wife was rebuked for her infidelity. 'If she is to return to her former sin, let her not now be healed: if she can keep from it, let her be healed.' The water broke out of her body and she was cured. The apostle brake bread and gave it her. She thanked God, believed with all her house, and relapsed no more into sin. Cratinus afterwards sent Andrew great gifts by his servants, and then, with his wife, asked him in person to accept them, but he refused saying: 'It is rather for you to give them to the needy.'

6 After this he went to Nicaea where were seven devils living among the tombs by the wayside, who at noon stoned passersby and had killed many. And all the city came out to meet Andrew with olive branches, crying: 'Our salvation is in thee, O man of God.' When they had told him all, he said: 'If you believe in Christ you shall be freed.' They cried: 'We will.' He thanked God and commanded the demons to appear; they came in the form of dogs. Said he: 'These are your enemies: if you profess your belief that I can drive them out in Jesus' name, I will do so.' They cried out: 'We believe that Jesus Christ whom thou preachest is the Son of God.' Then he bade the demons go into dry and barren places and hurt no man till the last day. They roared and vanished. The apostle baptized the people and made Callistus bishop.

7 At the gate of Nicomedia he met a dead man borne on a bier, and his old father supported by slaves, hardly able to walk, and his old mother

with hair torn, bewailing. 'How has it happened?' he asked. 'He was alone in his chamber and seven dogs rushed on him and killed him.' Andrew sighed and said: 'This is an ambush of the demons I banished from Nicaea. What will you do, father, if I restore your son?' 'I have nothing more precious than him, I will give him.' He prayed: 'Let the spirit of this lad return.' The faithful responded, 'Amen'. Andrew bade the lad rise, and he rose, and all cried: 'Great is the God of Andrew.' The parents offered great gifts which he refused, but took the lad to Macedonia, instructing him.

8 Embarking in a ship he sailed into the Hellespont, on the way to Byzantium. There was a great storm. Andrew prayed and there was calm. They reached Byzantium.

9 Thence proceeding through Thrace they met a troop of armed men who made as if to fall on them. Andrew made the sign of the cross against them, and prayed that they might be made powerless. A bright angel touched their swords and they all fell down, and Andrew and his company passed by while they worshipped him. And the angel departed in a great light.

10 At Perinthus he found a ship going to Macedonia, and an angel told him to go on board. As he preached the captain and the rest heard and were converted, and Andrew glorified God for making himself known on the sea.

11 At Philippi were two brothers, one of whom had two sons, the other two daughters. They were rich and noble, and said: 'There is no family as good as ours in the place: let us marry our sons to our daughters.' It was agreed and the earnest paid by the father of the sons. On the wedding-day a word from God came to them: 'Wait till my servant Andrew comes: he will tell you what you should do.' All preparations had been made, and guests bidden, but they waited. On the third day Andrew came: they went out to meet him with wreaths and told him how they had been charged to wait for him, and how things stood. His face was shining so that they marvelled at him. He said: 'Do not, my children, be deceived: rather repent, for you have sinned in thinking to join together those who

are near of kin. We do not forbid or shun marriage. It is a divine institution: but we condemn incestuous unions.' The parents were troubled and prayed for pardon. The young people saw Andrew's face like that of an angel, and said: 'We are sure that your teaching is true.' The apostle blessed them and departed.

12 At Thessalonica was a rich noble youth, Exoos, who came without his parents' knowledge and asked to be shown the way of truth. He was taught, and believed, and followed Andrew taking no care of his worldly estate. The parents heard that he was at Philippi and tried to bribe him with gifts to leave Andrew. He said: 'Would that you had not these riches, then would you know the true God, and escape his wrath.' Andrew, too, came down from the third storey and preached to them, but in vain: he retired and shut the doors of the house. They gathered a band and came to burn the house, saying: 'Death to the son who has forsaken his parents': and brought torches, reeds, and faggots, and set the house on fire. It blazed up. Exoos took a bottle of water and prayed: 'Lord Jesu Christ, in whose hand is the nature of all the elements, who moistenest the dry and driest the moist, coolest the hot and kindlest the quenched, put out this fire that thy servants may not grow evil, but be more enkindled unto faith.' He sprinkled the flames and they died. 'He is become a sorcerer,' said the parents, and got ladders, to climb up and kill them, but God blinded them. They remained obstinate, but one Lysimachus, a citizen, said: 'Why persevere? God is fighting for these. Desist, lest heavenly fire consume you.' They were touched, and said: 'This is the true God.' It was now night, but a light shone out, and they received sight. They went up and fell before Andrew and asked pardon, and their repentance made Lysimachus say: 'Truly Christ whom Andrew preaches is the Son of God.' All were converted except the youth's parents, who cursed him and went home again, leaving all their money to public uses. Fifty days after they suddenly died, and the citizens, who loved the youth, returned the property to him. He did not leave Andrew, but spent his income on the poor.

13 The youth asked Andrew to go with him to Thessalonica. All assembled in the theatre, glad to see their favourite. The youth preached to them, Andrew remaining silent, and all wondered at his wisdom. The

people cried out: 'Save the son of Carpianus who is ill, and we will believe.' Carpianus went to his house and said to the boy: 'You shall be cured today, Adimantus.' He said: 'Then my dream is come true: I saw this man in a vision healing me.' He rose up, dressed, and ran to the theatre, outstripping his father, and fell at Andrew's feet. The people seeing him walk after twenty-three years, cried: 'There is none like the God of Andrew.'

14 A citizen had a son possessed by an unclean spirit and asked for his cure. The demon, foreseeing that he would be cast out, took the son aside into a chamber and made him hang himself. The father said: 'Bring him to the theatre: I believe this stranger is able to raise him.' He said the same to Andrew. Andrew said to the people: 'What will it profit you if you see this accomplished and do not believe?' They said: 'Fear not, we will believe.' The lad was raised and they said: 'It is enough, we do believe.' And they escorted Andrew to the house with torches and lamps, for it was night, and he taught them for three days.

15 Medias of Philippi came and prayed for his sick son. Andrew wiped his cheeks and stroked his head, saying: 'Be comforted, only believe,' and went with him to Philippi. As they entered the city an old man met them and entreated for his sons, whom for an unspeakable crime Medias had imprisoned, and they were putrefied with sores. Andrew said: 'How can you ask help for your son when you keep these men bound? Loose their chains first, for your unkindness obstructs my prayers.' Medias, penitent, said: 'I will loose these two and seven others of whom you have not been told.' They were brought, tended for three days, cured, and freed. Then the apostle healed the son, Philomedes, who had been ill twenty-two years. The people cried: 'Heal our sick as well.' Andrew told Philomedes to visit them in their houses and bid them rise in the name of Jesus Christ, by which he had himself been healed. This was done, and all believed and offered gifts, which Andrew did not accept.

16 A citizen, Nicolaus, offered a gilt chariot and four white mules and four white horses as his most precious possession for the cure of his daughter. Andrew smiled. 'I accept your gifts, but not these visible ones:

if you offer this for your daughter, what will you for your soul? That is what I desire of you, that the inner man may recognize the true God, reject earthly things and desire eternal . . .' He persuaded all to forsake their idols, and healed the girl. His fame went through all Macedonia.

17 Next day as he taught, a youth cried out: 'What hast thou to do with us. Art thou come to turn us out of our own place?' Andrew summoned him: 'What is your work?' 'I have dwelt in this boy from his youth and thought never to leave him: but three days since I heard his father say, "I shall go to Andrew": and now I fear the torments thou bringest us and I shall depart.' The spirit left the boy. And many came and asked: 'In whose name dost thou cure our sick?'

Philosophers also came and disputed with him, and no one could resist his teaching.

18 At this time, one who opposed him went to the proconsul Virinus and said: 'A man is arisen in Thessalonica who says the temples should be destroyed and ceremonies done away, and all the ancient law abolished, and one God worshipped, whose servant he says he is.' The proconsul sent soldiers and knights to fetch Andrew. They found his dwelling: when they entered, his face so shone that they fell down in fear. Andrew told those present the proconsul's purpose. The people armed themselves against the soldiers, but Andrew stopped them. The proconsul arrived; not finding Andrew in the appointed place, he raged like a lion and sent twenty more men. They, on arrival, were confounded and said nothing. The proconsul sent a large troop to bring him by force. Andrew said: 'Have you come for me?' 'Yes, if you are the sorcerer who says the gods ought not to be worshipped.' 'I am no sorcerer, but the apostle of Jesus Christ whom I preach.' At this, one of the soldiers drew his sword and cried: 'What have I to do with thee, Virinus, that thou sendest me to one who can not only cast me out of this vessel, but burn me by his power? Would that you would come yourself! you would do him no harm.' And the devil went out of the soldier and he fell dead. On this came the proconsul and stood before Andrew but could not see him. 'I am he whom thou seekest.' His eyes were opened, and he said in anger: 'What is

this madness, that thou despisest us and our officers? Thou art certainly a sorcerer. Now will I throw thee to the beasts for contempt of our gods and us, and we shall see if the crucified whom thou preachest will help thee.' Andrew: 'Thou must believe, proconsul, in the true God and his Son whom he hath sent, specially now that one of thy men is dead.' And after long prayer he touched the soldier: 'Rise up: my God Jesus Christ raiseth thee.' He arose and stood whole. The people cried: 'Glory be to our God.' The proconsul: 'Believe not, O people, believe not the sorcerer.' They said: 'This is no sorcery but sound and true teaching.' The proconsul: 'I shall throw this man to the beasts and write about you to Caesar, that ye may perish for contemning his laws.' They would have stoned him, and said: 'Write to Caesar that the Macedonians have received the word of God, and forsaking their idols, worship the true God.'

Then the proconsul in wrath retired to the praetorium, and in the morning brought beasts to the stadium and had the Apostle dragged thither by the hair and beaten with clubs. First they sent in a fierce boar who went about him thrice and touched him not. The people praised God. A bull led by thirty soldiers and incited by two hunters, did not touch Andrew but tore the hunters to pieces, roared, and fell dead. 'Christ is the true God,' said the people. An angel was seen to descend and strengthen the apostle. The proconsul in rage sent in a fierce leopard, which left every one alone but seized and strangled the proconsul's son; but Virinus was so angry that he said nothing of it nor cared. Andrew said to the people: 'Recognize now that this is the true God, whose power subdues the beasts, though Virinus knows him not. But that ye may believe the more, I will raise the dead son, and confound the foolish father.' After long prayer, he raised him. The people would have slain Virinus, but Andrew restrained them, and Virinus went to the praetorium, confounded.

19 After this a youth who followed the apostle sent for his mother to meet Andrew. She came, and after being instructed, begged him to come to their house, which was devastated by a great serpent. As Andrew approached, it hissed loudly and with raised head came to meet him; it was fifty cubits long: every one fell down in fear. Andrew said: 'Hide thy head, foul one, which thou didst raise in the beginning for the hurt of

mankind, and obey the servants of God, and die.' The serpent roared, and coiled about a great oak nearby and vomited poison and blood and died.

Andrew went to the woman's farm, where a child killed by the serpent lay dead. He said to the parents: 'Our God who would have you saved hath sent me here that you may believe on him. Go and see the slayer slain.' They said: 'We care not so much for the child's death, if we be avenged.' They went, and Andrew said to the proconsul's wife: 'Go and raise the boy.' She went, nothing doubting, and said: 'In the name of my God Jesus Christ, rise up whole.' The parents returned and found their child alive, and fell at Andrew's feet.

20 On the next night he saw a vision which he related. 'Hearken, beloved, to my vision. I beheld, and lo, a great mountain raised up on high, which had on it nothing earthly, but only shone with such light, that it seemed to enlighten all the world. And lo, there stood by me my beloved brethren the apostles Peter and John; and John reached his hand to Peter and raised him to the top of the mount, and turned to me and asked me to go up after Peter, saying: "Andrew, thou art to drink Peter's cup." And he stretched out his hands and said: "Draw near to me and stretch out thy hands so as to join them unto mine, and put thy head by my head." When I did so I found myself shorter than John. After that he said to me: "Wouldst thou know the image of that which thou seest, and who it is that speaketh to thee?" and I said: "I desire to know it." And he said to me: "I am the word of the cross whereon thou shalt hang shortly, for his name's sake whom thou preachest." And many other things said he unto me, of which I must now say nothing, but they shall be declared when I come unto the sacrifice. But now let all assemble that have received the word of God, and let me commend them unto the Lord Jesus Christ, that he may vouchsafe to keep them unblemished in his teaching. For I am now being loosed from the body, and go unto that promise which he hath vouchsafed to promise me, who is the Lord of heaven and earth, the Son of God Almighty, very God with the Holy Ghost, continuing for everlasting ages.'

All the brethren wept and smote their faces. When all were gathered, Andrew said: 'Know, beloved, that I am about to leave you, but I trust in Jesus whose word I preach, that he will keep you from evil, that this harvest which I have sown among you may not be plucked up by the enemy, that is, the knowledge and teaching of my Lord Jesus Christ. But do ye pray always and stand firm in the faith, that the Lord may root out all tares of offence and vouchsafe to gather you into his heavenly garner as pure wheat.' So for five days he taught and confirmed them: then he spread his hands and prayed: 'Keep, I beseech thee, O Lord, this flock which hath now known thy salvation, that the wicked one may not prevail against it, but that what by thy command and my means it hath received, it may be able to preserve inviolate forever.' And all responded 'Amen'. He took bread, brake it with thanksgiving, gave it to all, saying: 'Receive the grace which Christ our Lord God giveth you by me his servant.' He kissed every one and commended them to the Lord, and departed to Thessalonica, and after teaching there two days, he left them.

21 Many faithful from Macedonia accompanied him in two ships. And all were desirous of being on Andrew's ship, to hear him. He said: 'I know your wish, but this ship is too small. Let the servants and baggage go in the larger ship, and you with me in this.' He gave them Anthimus to comfort them, and bade them go into another ship which he ordered to keep always near . . . that they might see him and hear the word of God. And as he slept a little, one fell overboard. Anthimus roused him, saying: 'Help us, good master; one of thy servants perisheth.' He rebuked the wind, there was a calm, and the man was borne by the waves to the ship. Anthimus helped him on board and all marvelled. On the twelfth day they reached Patrae in Achaia, disembarked, and went to an inn.

22 Many asked him to lodge with them, but he said he could only go where God bade him. That night he had no revelation, and the next night, being distressed at this, he heard a voice saying: 'Andrew, I am alway with thee and forsake thee not,' and was glad.

Lesbius the proconsul was told in a vision to take him in, and sent a messenger for him. He came, and entering the proconsul's chamber found him lying as dead with closed eyes; he struck him on the side and said: 'Rise and tell us what hath befallen thee.' Lesbius said: 'I abominated the way which you teach and sent soldiers in ships to the proconsul of Macedonia to send you bound to me, but they were wrecked and could not reach their destination. As I continued in my purpose of destroying your Way, two black men (Ethiopes) appeared and scourged me, saying: "We can no longer prevail here, for the man is coming whom you mean to persecute. So to-night, while we still have the power, we will avenge ourselves on you." And they beat me sorely and left me. But now do you pray that I may be pardoned and healed.' Andrew preached the word and all believed, and the proconsul was healed and confirmed in the faith.

23 Now Trophima, once the proconsul's mistress, and now married to another, left her husband and clave to Andrew. Her husband came to her lady (Lesbius' wife) and said she was renewing her liaison with the proconsul. The wife, enraged, said: 'This is why my husband has left me these six months.' She called her steward (procurator) and had Trophima sentenced as a prostitute and sent to the brothel. Lesbius knew nothing, and was deceived by his wife, when he asked about her. Trophima in the brothel prayed continually, and had the Gospel on her bosom, and no one could approach her. One day one offered her violence, and the Gospel fell to the ground. She cried to God for help and an angel came, and the youth fell dead. After that, she raised him, and all the city ran to the sight.

Lesbius' wife went to the bath with the steward, and as they bathed an ugly demon came and killed them both. Andrew heard and said: 'It is the judgement of God for their usage of Trophima.' The lady's nurse, decrepit from age, was carried to the spot, and supplicated for her. Andrew said to Lesbius: 'Will you have her raised?' 'No, after all the ill she has done.' 'We ought not to be unmerciful.' Lesbius went to the praetorium; Andrew raised his wife, who remained shamefaced: he bade her go home and pray. 'First', she said, 'reconcile me to Trophima whom I have injured.' 'She bears you no malice.' He called her and they were reconciled. Callisto was the wife.

Lesbius, growing in faith, came one day to Andrew and confessed all his sins. Andrew said: 'I thank God, my son, that thou fearest the judgement to come. Be strong in the Lord in whom thou believest.' And he took his hand and walked with him on the shore.

24 They sat down, with others, on the sand, and he taught. A corpse was thrown up by the sea near them. 'We must learn', said Andrew, 'what the enemy has done to him.' So he raised him, gave him a garment, and bade him tell his story. He said: 'I am the son of Sostratus, of Macedonia, lately come from Italy. On returning home I heard of a new teaching, and set forth to find out about it. On the way here we were wrecked and all drowned.' And after some thought, he realized that Andrew was the man he sought, and fell at his feet and said: 'I know that thou art the servant of the true God. I beseech thee for my companions, that they also may be raised and know him.' Then Andrew instructed him, and thereafter prayed God to show the bodies of the other drowned men: thirty-nine were washed ashore, and all there prayed for them to be raised. Philopator, the youth, said: 'My father sent me here with a great sum. Now he is blaspheming God and his teaching. Let it not be so.' Andrew ordered the bodies to be collected, and said: 'Whom will you have raised first?' He said: 'Warus my foster-brother.' So he was first raised and then the other thirty-eight. Andrew prayed over each, and then told the brethren each to take the hand of one and say: 'Jesus Christ the son of the living God raiseth thee.'

Lesbius gave much money to Philopator to replace what he had lost, and he abode with Andrew.

25 A woman, Calliopa, married to a murderer, had an illegitimate child and suffered in travail. She told her sister to call on Diana for help; when she did so the devil appeared to her at night and said: 'Why do you trouble me with vain prayers? Go to Andrew in Achaia.' She came, and he accompanied her to Corinth, Lesbius with him. Andrew said to Calliopa: 'You deserve to suffer for your evil life: but believe in Christ, and you will be relieved, but the child will be born dead.' And so it was.

26 Andrew did many signs in Corinth. Sostratus the father of Philopator, warned in a vision to visit Andrew, came first to Achaia and then to Corinth. He met Andrew walking with Lesbius, recognized him by his vision, and fell at his feet. Philopator said: 'This is my father, who seeks to know what he must do.' Andrew: 'I know that he is come to learn the truth; we thank God who reveals himself to believers.' Leontius the servant of Sostratus, said to him: 'Seest thou, sir, how this man's face shineth?' 'I see, my beloved,' said Sostratus; 'let us never leave him, but live with him and hear the words of eternal life.' Next day they offered Andrew many gifts, but he said: 'It is not for me to take aught of you but your own selves. Had I desired money, Lesbius is richer.'

27 After some days he bade them prepare him a bath; and going there saw an old man with a devil, trembling exceedingly. As he wondered at him, another, a youth, came out of the bath and fell at his feet, saying: 'What have we to do with thee, Andrew? Hast thou come here to turn us out of our abodes?' Andrew said to the people: 'Fear not,' and drove out both the devils. Then, as he bathed, he told them: 'The enemy of mankind lies in wait everywhere, in baths and in rivers; therefore we ought always to invoke the Lord's name, that he may have w power over us.'

They brought their sick to him to be healed, and so they did from other cities.

28 An old man, Nicolaus, came with clothes rent and said: 'I am seventy-four years old and have always been a libertine. Three days ago I heard of your miracles and teaching. I thought I would turn over a new leaf, and then again that I would not. in this doubt, I took a Gospel and prayed God to make me forget my old devices. A few days after, I forgot the Gospel I had about me, and went to the brothel. The woman said: "Depart, old man, depart: thou art an angel of God, touch me not nor approach me, for I see in thee a great mystery." Then I remembered the Gospel, and am come to you for help and pardon.' Andrew discoursed long against incontinence, and prayed from the sixth to the ninth hour. He rose and washed his face and said: 'I will not eat till I know if God will have mercy on this man.' A second day he fasted, but had no revelation

until the fifth day, when he wept vehemently and said: 'Lord, we obtain mercy for the dead, and now this man that desireth to know thy greatness, wherefore should he not return and thou heal him?' A voice from heaven said: 'Thou hast prevailed for the old man; but like as thou art worn with fasting, let him also fast, that he may be saved.' And he called him and preached abstinence. On the sixth day he asked the brethren all to pray for Nicolaus, and they did. Andrew then took food and permitted the rest to eat. Nicolaus went home, gave away all his goods, and lived for six months on dry bread and water. Then he died. Andrew was not there, but in the place where he was he heard a voice: 'Andrew, Nicolaus for whom thou didst intercede, is become mine.' And he told the brethren that Nicolaus was dead, and prayed that he might rest in peace.

29 And while he abode in that place (probably Lacedaemon) Antiphanes of Megara came and said: 'If there be in thee any kindness, according to the command of the Saviour whom thou preachest, show it now.' Asked what his story was, he told it. Returning from a journey, I heard the porter of my house crying out. They told me that he and his wife and son were tormented of a devil. I went upstairs and found other servants gnashing their teeth, running at me, and laughing madly. I went further up and found they had beaten my wife: she lay with her hair over her face unable to recognize me. Cure her, and I care nothing for the others.' Andrew said: 'There is no respect of persons with God. Let us go there.' They went from Lacedaemon to Megara, and when they entered the house, all the devils cried out: 'What dost thou here, Andrew? Go where thou art permitted: this house is ours.' He healed the wife and all the possessed persons, and Antiphanes and his wife became firm adherents.

30 He returned to Patrae where Egeas was now proconsul, and one Iphidamia, who had been converted by a disciple, Sosias, came and embraced his feet and said: 'My lady Maximilla who is in a fever has sent for you. The proconsul is standing by her bed with his sword drawn, meaning to kill himself when she expires.' He went to her, and said to Egeas: 'Do thyself no harm, but put up thy sword into his place. There will be a time when thou wilt draw it on me.' Egeas did not understand,

but made way. Andrew took Maximilla's hand, she broke into a sweat, and was well: he bade them give her food. The proconsul sent him 100 pieces of silver, but he would not look at them.

31 Going thence he saw a sick man lying in the dirt begging, and healed him.

32 Elsewhere he saw a blind man with wife and son, and said: 'This is indeed the devil's work: he has blinded them in soul and body.' He opened their eyes and they believed.

33 One who saw this said: 'I beg thee come to the harbour; there is a man, the son of a sailor, sick fifty years, cast out of the house, lying on the shore, incurable, full of ulcers and worms.' They went to him. The sick man said: 'Perhaps you are the disciple of that God who alone can save.' Andrew said: 'I am he who in the name of my God can restore thee to health,' and added: 'In the name of Jesus Christ, rise and follow me.' He left his filthy rags and followed, the pus and worms flowing from him. They went into the sea, and the apostle washed him in the name of the Trinity and he was whole, and ran naked through the city proclaiming the true God.

34 At this time the proconsul's brother Stratocles arrived from Italy. One of his slaves, Alcman, whom he loved, was taken by a devil and lay foaming in the court. Stratocles hearing of it said: 'Would the sea had swallowed me before I saw this.' Maximilla and Iphidamia said: 'Be comforted: there is here a man of God, let us send for him.' When he came he took the boy's hand and raised him whole. Stratocles believed and clave to Andrew.

35 Maximilla went daily to the praetorium and sent for Andrew to teach there. Egeas was away in Macedonia, angry because Maximilla had left him since her conversion. As they were all assembled one day, he returned, to their great terror. Andrew prayed that he might not be suffered to enter the place till all had dispersed. And Egeas was at once seized with indisposition, and in the interval the apostle signed them all

and sent them away, himself last. But Maximilla on the first opportunity came to Andrew and received the word of God and went home.

36 After this Andrew was taken and imprisoned by Egeans, and all came to the prison to be taught. After a few days he was scourged and crucified; he hung for three days, preaching, and expired, as is fully set forth in his Passion. Maximilla embalmed and buried his body.

37 From the tomb comes manna like flour, and oil: the amount shows the barrenness or fertility of the coming season -as I have told in my first book of Miracles. I have not set out his Passion at length, because I find it well done by some one else.

38 This much have I presumed to write, unworthy, unlettered, &c. The author's prayer for himself ends the book. May Andrew, on whose death-day he was born, intercede to save him.

Fragments

Of the detached fragments and quotations which precede the Passion there are three:

(a) One is in the Epistle of Titus.

When, finally, Andrew also [John has been cited shortly before] had come to a wedding, he too, to manifest the glory of God, disjoined certain who were intended to marry each other, men and women, and instructed them to continue holy in the single state.

No doubt this refers to the story in Gregory, ch. 11. Gregory, it may be noted, has altered the story (or has used an altered text), for the marriage of cousins was not forbidden till Theodosius' time (so Flamion). He or his source has imagined the relationship between the couples; in the original Acts none need have existed: the mere fact of the marriage was enough.

(b) The next are in a tract by Evodius, bishop of Uzala, against the Manichees:

Observe, in the Acts of Leucius which he wrote under the name of the apostles, what manner of things you accept about Maximilla the wife of Egetes: who, refusing to pay her due to her husband (though the apostle has said: Let the husband pay the due to the wife and likewise the wife to the husband: 1 Cor. vii. 3), imposed her maid Euclia upon her husband, decking her out, as is there written, with wicked (lit. hostile) enticements and paintings, and substituted her as deputy for herself at night, so that he in ignorance used her as his wife.

There also is it written, that when this same Maximilla and Iphidamia were gone together to hear the apostle Andrew, a beautiful child, who, Leucius would have us understand, was either God or at least an angel, escorted them to the apostle Andrew and went to the praetorium of Egetes, and entering their chamber feigned a woman's voice, as of

Maximilla, complaining of the sufferings of womankind, and of Iphidamia replying. When Egetes heard this dialogue, he went away. [These incidents must have intervened between cc. 35 and 36 of Gregory of Tours.]

(c) Evodius quotes another sentence, not certainly from the Acts of Andrew, but more in their manner than in that of John or Peter:

In the Acts written by Leucius, which the Manichees receive, it is thus written:

For the deceitful figments and pretended shows and collection (force, compelling) of visible things do not even proceed from their own nature, but from that man who of his own will has become worse through seduction.

It is obscure enough, in original and version: but is the kind of thing that would appeal to those who thought of material things and phenomena as evil.

We do not wonder that such narratives as that which Evodius quotes have been expunged, either by Gregory or his source, from the text.

The next passage is a fragment of some pages in length found by M. Bonnet in a Vatican MS. (Gr. 808) of tenth to eleventh century. There is no doubt that it is a piece of the original Acts. It is highly tedious in parts. Andrew in prison discourses to the brethren.

1 . . . is there in you altogether slackness? are ye not yet convinced of yourselves that ye do not yet bear his goodness? let us be reverent, let us rejoice with ourselves in the bountiful (ungrudging) fellowship which cometh of him. Let us say unto ourselves: Blessed is our race! by whom hath it been loved? blessed is our state! of whom hath it obtained mercy? we are not cast on the ground, we that have been recognized by so great highness: we are not the offspring of time, afterward to be dissolved by time; we are not a contrivance (product) of motion, made to be again destroyed by itself, nor things of earthly birth. ending again therein. We belong, then, to a greatness, unto which we aspire, of which we are the property, and peradventure to a greatness that hath mercy upon us. We

belong to the better; therefore we flee from the worse: we belong to the beautiful, for whose sake we reject the foul; to the righteous, by whom we cast away the unrighteous, to the merciful, by whom we reject the unmerciful; to the Saviour, by whom we recognize the destroyer; to the light, by whom we have cast away the darkness; to the One, by whom we have turned away from the many; to the heavenly, by whom we have learned to know the earthly; to the abiding, by whom we have seen the transitory. If we desire to offer unto God that hath had mercy on us a worthy thanksgiving or confidence or hymn or boasting, what better cause (theme) have we than that we have been recognized by him?

2 And having discoursed thus to the brethren, he sent them away every one to his house, saying to them: Neither are ye ever forsaken of me, ye that are servants of Christ, because of the love that is in him: neither again shall I be forsaken of you because of his intercession (mediation). And every one departed unto his house: and there was among them rejoicing after this sort for many days, while Aegeates took not thought to prosecute the accusation against the Apostle. Every one of them then was confirmed at that time in hope toward the Lord, and they assembled without fear in the prison, with Maximilla, Iphidamia, and the rest, continually, being sheltered by the protection and grace of the Lord.

3 But one day Aegeates, as he was hearing causes, remembered the matter concerning Andrew: and as one seized with madness, he left the cause which he had in hand, and rose up from the judgement seat and ran quickly to the praetorium, inflamed with love of Maximilla and desiring to persuade her with flatteries. And Maximilla was beforehand with him, coming from the prison and entering the house. And he went in and said to her:

4 Maximilla, thy parents counted me worthy of being thy consort, and gave me thine hand in marriage, not looking to wealth or descent or renown, but it may be to my good disposition of soul: and, that I may pass over much that I might utter in reproach of thee, both of that which I have enjoyed at thy parents' hands and thou from me during all our life, I am come, leaving the court, to learn of thee this one thing: answer me

then reasonably, if thou wert as the wife of former days, living with me in the way we know, sleeping, conversing, bearing offspring with me, I would deal well with thee in all points; nay more, I would set free the stranger whom I hold in prison: but if thou wilt not to thee I would do nothing harsh, for indeed I cannot; but him, whom thou affectionest more than me, I will afflict yet more. Consider, then, Maximilla, to whether of the two thou inclinest, and answer me to-morrow; for I am wholly armed for this emergency.

5 And with these words he went out; but Maximilla again at the accustomed hour, with Iphidamia, went to Andrew: and putting his hands before her own eyes, and then putting them to her mouth, she began to declare to him the whole rmatter of the demand of Aegeates. And Andrew answered her: I know, Maximilla my child, that thou thyself art moved to resist the whole attraction (promise) of nuptial union, desiring to be quit of a foul and polluted way of life: and this hath long been firmly held in thine (MS. mine) intention; but now thou wishest for the further testimony of mine opinion. I testify, O Maximilla: do it not; be not vanquished by the threat of Aegeates: be not overcome by his discourse: fear not his shameful counsels: fall not to his artful flatteries: consent not to surrender thyself to his impure spells, but endure all his torments looking unto us for a little space, and thou shalt see him wholly numbed and withering away from thee and from all that are akin to thee. But (For) that which I most needed to say to thee -for I rest not till I fulfil the business which is seen, and which cometh to pass in thy person- hath escaped me: and rightly in thee do I behold Eve repenting, and in myself Adam returning; for that which she suffered in ignorance, thou now (for whose soul I strive) settest right by returning: and that which the spirit suffered which was overthrown with her and slipped away from itself, is set right in me, with thee who seest thyself being brought back. For her defect thou hast remedied by not suffering like her; and his imperfection I have perfected by taking refuge with God, that which she disobeyed thou hast obeyed: that whereto he consented I flee from: and that which they both transgressed we have been aware of, for it is ordained that every one should correct (and raise up again) his own fall.

6 I, then, having said this as I have said it, would go on to speak as followeth: Well done, O nature that art being saved for thou hast been strong and hast not hidden thyself (from God like Adam)! Well done, O soul that criest out of what thou hast surfered, and returnest unto thyself ! Well done, O man that understandest what is thine and dost press on to what is thine! Well done, thou that hearest what is spoken, for I see thee to be greater than things that are thought or spoken! I recognize thee as more powerful than the things which seemed to overpower thee; as more beautiful than those which cast thee down into foulness, which brought thee down into captivity. Perceiving then, O man, all this in thyself, that thou art immaterial, holy light, akin to him that is unborn, that thou art intellectual, heavenly, translucent, pure, above the flesh, above the world, above rulers, above principalities, over whom thou art in truth, then comprehend thyself in thy condition and receive full knowledge and understand wherein thou excellest: and beholding thine own face in thine essence, break asunder all bonds -I say not only those that are of thy birth, but those that are above birth, whereof we have set forth to thee the names which are excecding great -desire earnestly to see him that is revealed unto thee, him who doth not come into being, whom perchance thou alone shalt recognize with confidence.

7 These things have I spoken of thee, Maximilla, for in their meaning the things I have spoken reach unto thee. Like as Adam died in Eve because he consented unto her confession, so do I now live in thee that keepest the Lord's commandment and stablishest thyself in the rank (dignity) of thy being. But the threats of Aegeates do thou trample down, Maximilla, knowing that we have God that hath mercy on us. And let not his noise move thee, but continue chaste- and let him punish me not only with such torments as bonds, but let him cast me to the beasts or burn me with fire, and throw me from a precipice. And what need I say? there is but this one body; let him abuse that as he will, for it is akin to himself.

8 And yet again unto thee is my speech, Maximilla: I say unto thee, give not thyself over unto Aegeates: withstand his ambushes- for indeed, Maximilla, I have seen my Lord saying unto me: Andrew, Aegeates' father the devil will loose thee from this prison. Thine, therefore, let it be

henceforth to keep thyself chaste and pure, holy, unspotted, sincere, free from adultery, not reconciled to the discourses of our enemy, unbent, unbroken, tearless, unwounded, not storm-tossed, undivided, not stumbling without fellow-feeling for the works of Cain. For if thou give not up thyself, Maximilla, to what is contrary to these, I also shall rest, though I be thus forced to leave this life for thy sake that is, for mine own. But if I were thrust out hence, even I, who, it may be, might avail through thee to profit others that are akin to me, and if thou wert persuaded by the discourse of Aegeates and the flatteries of his father the serpent, so that thou didst turn unto thy former works, know thou that on thine account I should be tormented until thou thyself sawest that I had contemned life for the sake of a soul which was not worthy.

9 I entreat, therefore, the wise man that is in thee that thy mind continue clear seeing. I entreat thy mind that is not seen, that it be preserved whole: I beseech thee, love thy Jesus, and yield not unto the worse. Assist me, thou whom I entreat as a man, that I may become perfect: help me also, that thou mayest recognize thine own true nature: feel with me in my suffering, that thou mayest take knowledge of what I suffer, and escape suffering see that which I see, and thou shalt be blind to what thou seest: see that which thou shouldst, and thou shalt not see that thou shouldst not: hearken to what I say, and cast away that which thou hast heard.

10 These things have I spoken unto thee and unto every one that heareth, if he will hear. But thou, O Stratocles, said he, looking toward him, Why art thou so oppressed, with many tears and groanings to be heard afar off? what is the lowness of spirit that is on thee? why thy much pain and thy great anguish? dost thou take note of what is said, and wherefore I pray thee to be disposed in mind as my child? (or, my child, to be composed in mind): dost thou perceive unto whom my words are spoken? hath each of them taken hold on thine understanding? have they whetted (MS. touched) thine intellectual part? have I thee as one that hath hearkened to me? do I find myself in thee? is there in thee one that speaketh whom I see to be mine own? doth he love him that speaketh in me and desire to have fellowship with him? doth he wish to be made one

with him? doth lie hasten to become his friend? doth he yearn to be joined with him? doth he find in him any rest? hath he where to lay his head? doth nought oppose him there? nought that is wroth with him, resisteth him, hateth him, fleeth from him, is savage, avoideth, turneth away, starteth off, is burdened, maketh war, talketh with others, is flattered by others, agreeth with others? Doth nothing else disturb him? Is there one within that is strange to me? an adversary, a breaker of peace, an enemy, a cheat, a sorcerer, a crooked dealer, unsound, guileful, a hater of men, a hater of the word, one like a tyrant, boastful, puffed up, mad, akin to the serpent, a weapon of the devil, a friend of the fire, belonging to darkness? Is there in thee any one, Stratocles, that cannot endure my saying these things? Who is it? Answer: do I talk in vain? have I spoken in vain? Nay, saith the man in thee, Stratocles, who now again weepeth.

11 And Andrew took the band of Stratocles and said: I have him whom I loved; I shall rest on him whom I look for; for thy yet groaning, and weeping without restraint, is a sign unto me that I have already found rest, that I have not spoken to thee these words which are akin to me, in vain.

12 And Stratocles answered him: Think not, most blessed Andrew, that there is aught else that afflicteth me but thee; for the words that come forth of thee are like arrows of fire shot against me, and every one of them reacheth me and verily burneth me up. That part of my soul which inclineth to what I hear is tormented, divining the affliction that is to follow, for thou thyself departest, and, I know, nobly: but hereafter when I seek thy care and affection, where shall I find it, or in whom? I have received the seeds of the words of salvation, and thou wast the sower: but that they should sprout up and grow needs none other but thee, most blessed Andrew. And what else have I say to thee but this? I need much mercy and help from thee, to become worthy of the seed I have from thee, which will not otherwise increase perpetually or grow up into the light except thou willest it, and prayest for them and for the whole of me.

13 And Andrew answered him: This, my child, was what I beheld in thee myself. And I glorify my Lord that my thought of thee walked not

on the void, but knew what it said. But that ye may know the truth, tomorrow doth Aegeates deliver me up to be crucified: for Maximilla the servant of the Lord will enrage the enemy that is in him, unto whom he belongeth, by not consenting to that which is hateful to her; and by turning against me he will think to console himself.

14 Now while the apostle spake these things, Maximilla was not there, for she having heard throughout the words wherewith he answered her, and being in part composed by them, and of such a mind as the words pointed out, set forth not inadvisedly nor without purpose and went to the praetorium. And she bade farewell to all the life of the flesh, and when Aegeates brought to her the same demand which he had told her to consider, whether she would lie with him, she rejected it- and thenceforth he bent himself to putting Andrew to death, and thought to what death he should expose him. And when of all deaths crucifixion alone prevailed with him, he went away with his like and dined; and Maximilla, the Lord going before her in the likeness of Andrew, with Iphidamia came back to the prison- and there being therein a great gathering of the brethren, she found Andrew discoursing thus:

15 I, brethren, was sent forth by the Lord as an apostle unto these regions whereof my Lord thought me worthy, not to teach any man, but to remind every man that is akin to such words that they live in evils which are temporal, delighting in their injurious delusions: wherefrom I have always exhorted you also to depart, and encouraged you to press toward things that endure, and to take flight from all that is transitory (flowing)- for ye see that none of you standeth, but that all things, even to the customs of men, are easily changeable. And this befalleth because the soul is untrained and erreth toward nature and holdeth pledges toft its error. I therefore account them blessed who have become obedient unto the word preached, and thereby see the mysteries of their own nature; for whose sake all things have been builded up.

16 I enjoin you therefore, beloved children, build yourselves firmly upon the foundation that hath been laid for you, which is unshaken, and against which no evil- willer can conspire. Be then, rooted upon this

foundation: be established, remembering what ye have seen (or heard) and all that hath come to pass while I walked with you all. Ye have seen works wrought through me which ye have no power to disbelieve, and such signs come to pass as perchance even dumb nature will proclaim aloud; I have delivered you words which I pray may so be received by you as the words themselves would have it. Be established then, beloved upon all that ye have seen, and heard, and partaken of. And God on whom ye have believed shall have mercy on you and present you lmto himself, giving you rest unto all ages.

17 Now as for that which is to befall me, let it not really trouble you as some strange spectacle, that the servant of God unto whom God himself hath granted much in deeds and words, should by an evil man be driven out of this temporal life: for not only unto me will this come to pass, but unto all them that have loved and believed on him and confess him. The devil that is wholly shameless will arm his own children against them, that they may consent unto him; and he will not have his desire. And wherefore he essayeth this I will tell you. From the beginning of all things, and if I may so say, since he that hath no beginning came down to be under his rule, the enemy that is a foe to peace driveth away from (God) such a one as doth not belong indeed to him, but is some one of the weaker sort and not fully enlightened (?), nor yet able to recognize himself. And because he knoweth him not, therefore must he be fought against by him (the devil). For he, thinking that he possesseth him and is his master for ever, opposeth him so much, that he maketh their enmity to be a kind of friendship: for suggesting to him his own thoughts, he often portrayeth them as pleasurable and specious (MS. deceitful), by which he thinketh to prevail over him. He was not, then, openly shown to be an enemy, for he feigned a friendship that was worthy of him.

18 And this his work he carried on so long that he (man) forgat to recognize it, but he (the devil) knew it himself: that is, he, because of his gifts . But when the mystery of grace was lighted up, and the counsel of rest manifested, and the light of the word shown, and the race of them that were saved was proved, warring against many pleasures, [he, seeing] the enemy himself despised, and himself, through the goodness of him

that had mercy on us, derided because of his own gifts, by which he had thought to triumph over man- he began to plot against us with hatred and enmity and assaults; and this hath he dctcrmined, not to cease from us till he thinketh to separate us (from God).

For before, our enemy was without care, and offered us a feigned friendship which was worthy of him, and was able not to fear that we, deceived by him, should depart from him. But when the light of dispensation was kindled, it made , I say not stronger, . For it exposed that part of his nature which was hidden and which thought to escape notice, and made it confess what it is.

Knowing therefore, brethren, that which shall be, let us be vigilant, not discontented, not making a proud figure, not carrying upon our souls marks of him which are not our own: but wholly lifted upward by the whole word, let us all gladly await the end, and take our flight away from him, that he may be henceforth shown as he is, who our nature unto (or against) our . . .

The Martyrdom

The original text of this, as Flamion shows, has to be picked out of several Greek and Latin authorities.

Bonnet prints the Martyrdom in several forms (Act. Apost. Apocr. ii. 1): on pp. 1-37 we have the Passion in three texts.

The uppermost is the Latin letter of the presbyters and deacons of Achaia. This, as Bonnet has proved, is the original of the two Greek versions printed below it. The first editors of this Letter thought it might be a genuine document. But it is really an artificial thing. The greater part of it consists of a dialogue between Andrew and Aegeates: the narrative of the actual Passion is rather brief.

Of the two Greek versions, the first, which begins "ha tois ophthalmois"(greek) is a faithful version of the Latin.

The other, which begins "haper tois ophthalmois"(greek) has a number of insertions taken from the original Acts, ultimately, perhaps through the medium of a 'Passion', circulated separately, such as we have had in the cases of John, Paul, and Peter. This text is called by Flamion the Epitre grecque. Ep. gr.

On pp. 38-45 follows the fragment of discourses which has just been translated. Very likely this is a relic of a separate Passion cut off from the end of the original Acts.

On pp. 46-57 is the 'Martyrium prius'. This tells (after speaking of the dispersion of the apostles) of the cure and conversion of Lesbius, destruction of temples, dismissal of Lesbius by Caesar, vision of Andrew that Aegeates is to put him to death, arrest of Andrew, and martyrdom. It contains many speeches. This is Mart. 1.

On pp. 58-64 is the 'Martyrium alterum' in two texts, which begins at once with the arrest of the apostle by Aegeates- after he has spent the night in discoursing to the brethren.

Mart. II, A, B are the two texts of this. Besides these Bonnet has published in the Analecta Bollandiana and separately (as Supplementum Codicis Apocryphi, ii, 1895) the following documents:

1 Acts of Andrew with Encomium: called for short Laudatio, which recounts the journeys at considerable length, and some of the miracles which we have seen in Gregory, and then the Passion (cc. 44-9) and the Translation to Constantinople.

2. A Greek Martyrdom, of which cc. 1-8 recount the journeys, and from 9 onwards the Passion, with a good deal of matter from the original Acts. This is called Narratio.

3. A Latin Passion- that known to Gregory, which begins Conversante et docente: it forms the end of Book III of Abdias' Historia Apostolica, and is there tacked on to Gregory's book of Miracles.

Using all these sources, Flamion has with great pains indicated which portions he assigns to the original Acts, and I shall follow him here. The resultant text is a kind of mosaic, of which the sources shall be indicated in the margin.

And after he had thus discoursed throughout the night to the brethren, and prayed with them and committed them unto the Lord, early in the morning Aegeates the proconsul sent for the apostle Andrew out of the prison and said to him: The end of thy judgement is at hand, thou stranger, enemy of this present life and foe of all mine house. Wherefore hast thou thought good to intrude into places that are not thine, and to corrupt my wife who was of old obedient unto me? why hast thou done this against me and against all Achaia ? Therefore shalt thou receive from me a gift in recompense of that thou hast wrought against me.

And he commanded him to be scourged by seven men and afterward to be crucified: and charged the executioners that his legs should be left unpierced, and so he should be hanged up: thinking by this means to torment him the more.

Now the report was noised throughout all Patrae that the stranger, the righteous man, the servant of Christ whom Aegeates held prisoner, was being crucified, having done nothing amiss: and they ran together with one accord unto the sight, being wroth with the proconsul because of his impious judgement.

And as the executioners led him unto the place to fulfil that which was commanded them, Stratocles heard what was come to pass, and ran hastily and overtook them, and beheld the blessed Andrew violently haled by the executioners like a malefactor. And he spared them not, but beating every one of them soundly and tearing their coats from top to bottom, he caught Andrew away from them, saying: Ye may thank the blessed man who hath instructed me and taught me to refrain from extremity of wrath: for else I would have showed you what Stratocles is able to do, and what is the power of the foul Aegeates. For we have learnt to endure that which others inflict upon us. And he took the hand of the apostle and went with him to the place by the sea-shore where he was to be crucified.

But the soldiers who had received him from the proconsul left him with Stratocles, and returned and told Aegeates, saying: As we went with Andrew Stratocles prevented us, and rent our coats and pulled him away from us and took him with him, and lo, here we are as thou seest. And Aegeates answered them: Put on other raiment and go and fulfil that which I commanded you, upon the condemned man: but be not seen of Stratocles, neither answer him again if he ask aught of you; for I know the rashness of his soul, what it is, and if he were provoked he would not even spare me. And they did as Aegeates said unto them.

But as Stratocles went with the apostle unto the place appointed, Andrew perceived that he was wroth with Aegeates and was reviling him in a low voice, and said unto him: My child Stratocles, I would have thee henceforth possess thy soul unmoved, and remove from thyself this temper, and neither be inwardly disposed thus toward the things that seem hard to thee, nor be inflamed outwardly: for it becometh the servant of Jesus to be worthy of Jesus. And another thing will I say unto thee and to the brethren that walk with me: that the man that is against us, when he dareth aught against us and findeth not one to consent unto him, is smitten and beaten and wholly deadened because he hath not accomplished that which he undertook; let us therefore, little children, have him alway before our eyes, lest if we fall asleep he slaughter us (you) like an adversary.

And as he spake this and yet more unto Stratocles and them that were with him, they came to the place where he was to be crucified: and (seeing the cross set up at the edge of the sand by the sea-shore) he left them all and went to the cross and spake unto it (as unto a living creature, with a loud voice):

Hail, O cross, yea be glad indeed! Well know I that thou shalt henceforth be at rest, thou that hast for a long time been wearied, being set up and awaiting me. I come unto thee whom I know to belong to me. I come unto thee that hast yearned after me. I know thy mystery, for the which thou art set up: for thou art planted in the world to establish the things that are unstable: and the one part of thee stretcheth up toward heaven that thou mayest signify the heavenly word (or, the word that is above) (the head of all things): and another part of thee is spread out to the right hand and the left that it may put to flight the envious and adverse power of the evil one, and gather into one the things that are scattered abroad (or, the world): And another part of thee is planted in the earth, and securely set in the depth, that thou mayest join the things that are in the earth and that are under the earth unto the heavenly things (Laud. that thou mayest draw up them that be under the earth and them that are held in the places beneath the earth, and join, &c.).

O cross, device (contrivance) of the salvation of the Most High! O cross, trophy of the victory [of Christ] over the enemies! O cross, planted upon the earth and having thy fruit in the heavens! O name of the cross, filled with all things (lit. a thing filled with all).

Well done, O cross, that hast bound down the mobility of the world (or, the circumference)! Well done, O shape of understanding that hast shaped the shapeless (earth?)! Well done, O unseen chastisement that sorely chastisest the substance of the knowledge that hath many gods, and drivest out from among mankind him that devised it! Well done, thou that didst clothe thyself with the Lord, and didst bear the thief as a fruit, and didst call the apostle to repentance, and didst not refuse to accept us!

But how long delay I, speaking thus, and embrace not the cross, that by the cross I may be made alive, and by the cross (win) the common death of all and depart out of life?

Come hitller ye ministers of joy unto me, ye servants of Aegeates: accomplish the desire of us both, and bind the lamb unto the wood of suffering, the man unto the maker, the soul unto the Saviour.

And the blessed Andrew having thus spoken, standing upon the earth, looked earnestly upon the cross, and bade the brethren that the executioners should come and do that which was commanded them; for they stood afar off.

And they came and bound his hands and his feet and nailed them not; for such a charge had they from Aegeates; for he wished to afflict him by hanging him up, and that in the night he might be devoured alive by dogs (Laud. that he might be wearied out and permit Maximilla to live with him). And they left him hanging and departed from him.

And when the multitudes that stood by of them that had been made disciples in Christ by him saw that they had done unto him none of the things accustomed with them that are crucified, they hoped to hear something again from him. For as he hung, he moved his head and smiled. And Stratocles asked him, saying: Wherefore smilest thou, servant of God? thy laughter maketh us to mourn and weep because we are bereaved of thee. And the blessed Andrew answered him: Shall I not laugh, my son Stratocles, at the vain assault (ambush) of Aegeates, whereby he thinketh to punish us? we are strangers unto him and his conspiracics. He hath not to hear; for if he had, he would have heard that the man of Jesus cannot be punished, because he is henceforth known of him.

And thereafter he spake unto them all in common, for the heathen also were come together, being wroth at the unjust judgement of Aegeates.

Ye men that are here present, and women and children, old and young, bond and free, and all that will hear, take ye no heed of the vain deceit of this present life, but heed us rather who hang here for the Lord's sake and are about to depart out of this body: and renounce all the lusts of the world and contemn (spit upon) the worship of the abominable idols, and run unto the true worshipping of our God that lieth not, and make yourselves a temple pure and ready to receive the word. (Narr. then becomes obviously late: Ep. Gr., which is far shorter, ends: And hasten to overtake my soul as it hasteneth toward heavenly things, and in a word despise all temporal things, and establish your minds as men believing in Christ.)

And the multitudes hearing the things which he spake departed not from the place; and Andrew continued speaking yet more unto them, for a day and a night. And on the day following, beholding his endurance and constancy of soul and wisdom of spirit and strength of mind, they were wroth, and hastened with one accord unto Aegeates, to the judgement-seat where he sat, and cried out against him, saying: What is this judgement of thine, O proconsul ? thou hast ill judged! thou hast condemned unjustly: thy court is against law! What evil hath this man done? wherein hath he offended? The city is troubled: thou injurest us all! destroy not Caesar's city! give us the righteous man! restore us the holy man! slay not a man dear to God! destroy not a man gentle and pious! lo, two days is he hanged up and yet liveth, and hath tasted nothing, and yet refresheth all us with his words, and lo, we believe in the God whom he preacheth. Take down the righteous man and we will all turn philosophers; loose the chaste man and all Patrae will be at peace, set free the wise man and all Achaia shall be set free by him! (or, obtain mercy.)

But when at the first Aegeates would not hear them, but beckoned with the hand to the people that they should depart, they were filled with rage and were at the point to do him violence, being in number about two thousand (Narr., Ep. Gr., Mart. II: 20,000).

And when the proconsul saw them to be after a sort mad, he feared lest there should be a rising against him, and rose up from the judgement-seat and went with them, promising to release Andrew. And some went before and signified to the apostle and to the rest of the people that were there, wherefore the proconsul was coming. And all the multitude of the disciples rejoiced together with Maximilla and Iphidamia and Stratocles.

But when Andrew heard it, he began to say: O the dullness and disobedience and simplicity of them whom I have taught! how much have I spoken, and even to this day I have not persuaded them to flee from the love of earthly things! but they are yet bound unto them and continue in them, and will not depart from them. What meaneth this affection and love and sympathy with the flesh? how long heed ye worldly and temporal things? how long understand ye not the things that be above us, and press not to overtake them? Ieave me henceforth to be put to death in the manner which ye behold, and let no man by any means loose me from these bonds, for so is it appointed unto me to depart out of the body and be present with the Lord, with whom also I am crucified. And this shall be accomplished.

And he turned unto Aegeates and said with a loud voice: Wherefore art thou come, Aegeates, that art an alien unto me? what wilt thou dare afresh, what contrive, or what fetch? tell us that thou hast repented and art come to loose us? nay, not if thou repentest, indeed, Aegeates, will I now consent unto thee, not if thou promise me all thy substance will I depart from myself, not if thou say that thou art mine will I trust thee. And dost thou, proconsul, loose him that is bound? him that hath been set free? that hath been recognized by his kinsman? that hath obtained mercy and is beloved of him? dost thou loose him that is alien to thee? the stranger? that only appeareth to thee? I have one with whom I shall be for ever, with whom I shall converse for unnumbered ages. Unto him do I go, unto him do I hasten, who made thee also known unto me, who said to me: Understand thou Aegeates and his gifts let not that fearful one afright thee, nor think that he holdeth thee who art mine. He is thine enemy: he is pestilent, a deceiver, a corrupter, a madman, a sorcerer, a cheat, a murderer, wrathful, without compassion. Depart therefore from me, thou worker of all iniquity. (Ep. Gr. He is thine enemy. Therefore I know thee, through him that permitted me to know. I depart from thee. For I and they that are akin to me hasten toward that which is ours, and leave thee to be what thou wast, and what thou knowest not thyself to be.)

And the Proconsul hearing this stood speechless and as it were beside himself; but as all the city made an e uproar that he should loose Andrew, he drew near to the cross to loose him and take him down. But the blessed Andrew cried out with a loud voice: Suffer not Lord, thine Andrew that hath been bound upon thy cross, to be loosed again; give not me that am upon thy mystery to the shameless devil; O Jesu Christ, let not thine adversary loose him that is hung upon thy grace; O Father, let not this mean (little) one humble any more him that hath known thy greatness. But do thou, Jesu Christ, whom I have seen, whom I hold, whom I love, in whom I am and shall be, receive me in peace into thine everlasting tabernacles, that by my going out there may be an entering in unto thee of many that are akin to me, and that they may rest in thy majesty. And having so said, and yet more glorified the Lord, he gave up the ghost, while we all wept and lamented at our parting from him.

And after the decease of the blessed Andrew, Maximilla together with Stratocles, caring nought for them that stood by, drew near and herself loosed his body: and when it was evening she paid it the accustomed care and buried it (hard by the sea-shore). And she continued separate from Aegeates because of his brutal soul and his wicked manner of life: and she led a reverend and quiet life, filled with the love of Christ, among the brethren. Whom Aegeates solicited much, and promised that she should have the rule over his affairs; but being unable to persuade her, he arose in the dead of night and unknown to them of his house cast himself down from a great height and perished.

But Stratocles, which was his brother after the flesh, would not touch aught of the things that were left of his substance; for the wretched man died without offspring: but said: Let thy goods go with thee, Aegeates.

For of these things we have no need, for they are polluted; but for me, let Christ be my friend and I his servant, and all my substance do I offer unto him in whom I have believed, and I pray that by worthy hearing of the blessed teaching of the apostle I may appear a partaker with him in the ageless and unending kingdom. And so the uproar of the people ceased, and all were glad at the amazing and untimely and sudden fall of the impious and lawless Aegeates.

The Acts of Andrew

What we have all, both presbyters and deacons of the churches of Achaia, beheld with our eyes, we have written to all the churches established in the name of Christ Jesus, both in the east and west, north and south. Peace to you, and to all who believe in one God, perfect Trinity, true Father unbegotten, true Son only-begotten, true Holy Spirit proceeding from the Father, and abiding in the Son, in order that there may be shown one Holy Spirit subsisting in the Father and Son in precious Godhead. This faith we have learned from the blessed Andrew, the apostle of our Lord Jesus Christ, whose passion also we, having seen it set forth before our eyes, have not hesitated to give an account of, according to the degree of ability we have.

Accordingly the proconsul Ægeates, having come into the city of Patras, began to compel those believing in Christ to worship the idols; to whom the blessed Andrew, running up, said: It behooved you, being a judge of men, to acknowledge your Judge who is in the heaven, and having acknowledged Him, to worship Him; and worshipping Him who is the true God, to turn away your thoughts from those which are not true gods.

To whom Ægeates said: Are you Andrew, who destroyest the temples of the gods, and persuadest men about the religion which, having lately made its appearance, the emperors of the Romans have given orders to suppress?

The blessed Andrew said: The emperors of the Romans have never recognised the truth. And this the Son of God, who came on account of the salvation of men, manifestly teaches— that these idols are not only not gods, but also most shameful demons, and hostile to the human race, teaching men to offend God, so that, by being offended, He turns away and will not hearken; that therefore, by His turning away and not hearkening, they may be held captive by the devil; and that they might work them to such a degree, that when they go out of the body they may be found deserted and naked, carrying nothing with them but sins.

Ægeates said: These are superfluous and vain words: as for your Jesus, for proclaiming these things to the Jews they nailed him to the tree of the cross.

The blessed Andrew answering, said: Oh, if you would recognise the mystery of the cross, with what reasonable love the Author of the life of the human race for our restoration endured this tree of the cross, not unwillingly, but willingly!

Ægeates said: Seeing that, betrayed by his own disciple, and seized by the Jews, he was brought before the procurator, and according to their request was nailed up by the procurator's soldiers, in what way do you say that he willingly endured the tree of the cross?

The holy Andrew said: For this reason I say willingly, since I was with Him when he was betrayed by His disciple. For before He was betrayed, He spoke to us to the effect that He should be betrayed and crucified for the salvation of men, and foretold that He should rise again on the third day. To whom my brother Peter said, (Matthew 16:22) Far be it from you, Lord; let this by no means be. And so, being angry, He said to Peter, Get behind me, Satan; for you are not disposed to the things of God. And in order that He might most fully explain that He willingly underwent the passion, He said to us, (John 10:18) I have power to lay down my life, and I have power to take it again. And, last of all, while He was supping with us, He said, (Matthew 26:21) One of you will betray me. At these words, therefore, all becoming exceedingly grieved, in order that the surmise might be free from doubt, He made it clear, saying, To whomsoever I shall give the piece of bread out of my hand, he it is who betrays me. When, therefore, He gave it to one of our fellow disciples, and gave an account of things to come as if they were already present, He showed that He was to be willingly betrayed. For neither did He run away, and leave His betrayer at fault; but remaining in the place in which He knew that he was, He awaited him.

Ægeates said: I wonder that you, being a sensible man, should wish to uphold him on any terms whatever; for, whether willingly or unwillingly, all the same, you admit that he was fastened to the cross.

The blessed Andrew said: This is what I said, if now you apprehend, that great is the mystery of the cross, which, if you wish, as is likely, to hear, attend to me.

Ægeates said: A mystery it cannot be called, but a punishment.

The blessed Andrew said: This punishment is the mystery of man's restoration. If you will listen with any attention, you will prove it.

Ægeates said: I indeed will hear patiently; but you, unless you submissively obey me, shall receive the mystery of the cross in yourself.

The blessed Andrew answered: If I had been afraid of the tree of the cross, I should not have proclaimed the glory of the cross.

Ægeates said: Your speech is foolish, because you proclaim that the cross is not a punishment, and through your foolhardiness you are not afraid of the punishment of death.

The holy Andrew said: It is not through foolhardiness, but through faith, that I am not afraid of the punishment of death; for the death of sins is hard. And on this account I wish you to hear the mystery of the cross, in order that you perhaps, acknowledging it, may believe, and believing, may come somehow or other to the renewing of your soul.

Ægeates said: That which is shown to have perished is for renewing. Do you mean that my soul has perished, that you make me come to the renewing of it through the faith, I know not what, of which you have spoken?

The blessed Andrew answered: This it is which I desired time to learn, which also I shall teach and make manifest, that though the souls of men are destroyed, they shall be renewed through the mystery of the cross. For the first man through the tree of transgression brought in death; and it was necessary for the human race, that through the suffering of the tree, death, which had come into the world, should be driven out. And since the first man, who brought death into the world through the transgression of the tree, had been produced from the spotless earth, it was necessary that the Son of God should be begotten a perfect man from the spotless virgin, that He should restore eternal life, which men had lost through Adam, and should cut off the tree of carnal appetite through the tree of the cross. Hanging upon the cross, He stretched out His blameless hands for the hands which had been incontinently stretched out; for the most sweet food of the forbidden tree He received gall for food; and taking our mortality upon Himself, He made a gift of His immortality to us.

Ægeates said: With these words you shall be able to lead away those who shall believe in you; but unless you have come to grant me this, that you offer sacrifices to the almighty gods, I shall order you, after having been scourged, to be fastened to that very cross which you commend.

The blessed Andrew said: To God Almighty, who alone is true, I bring sacrifice day by day; not the smoke of incense, nor the flesh of bellowing bulls, nor the blood of goats, but sacrificing a spotless lamb day by day on the altar of the cross; and though all the people of the faithful partake of His body and drink His blood, the Lamb that has been sacrificed remains after this entire and alive. Truly, therefore, is He sacrificed, and truly is His body eaten by the people, and His blood is likewise drunk; nevertheless, as I have said, He remains entire, and spotless, and alive.

Ægeates said: How can this be?

The blessed Andrew said: If you would know, take the form of a disciple, that you may learn what you are inquiring after.

Ægeates said: I will exact of you through tortures the gift of this knowledge.

The blessed Andrew declared: I wonder that you, being an intelligent man, should fall into the folly of thinking that you may be able to persuade me, through your tortures, to disclose to you the sacred things of God. You have heard the mystery of the cross, you have heard the mystery of the sacrifice. If you believe in Christ the Son of God, who was crucified, I shall altogether disclose to you in what manner the Lamb that has been slain may live, after having been sacrificed and eaten, remaining in His kingdom entire and spotless.

Ægeates said: And by what means does the lamb remain in his kingdom after he has been slain and eaten by all the people, as you have said?

The blessed Andrew said: If you believe with all your heart, you shall be able to learn: but if you believe not, you shall not by any means attain to the idea of such truth.

Then Ægeates, enraged, ordered him to be shut up in prison, where, when he was shut up, a multitude of the people came together to him from almost all the province, so that they wished to kill Ægeates, and by breaking down the doors of the prison to set free the blessed Andrew the apostle.

Them the blessed Andrew admonished in these words, saying: Do not stir up the peace of our Lord Jesus Christ into seditious and devilish uproar. For my Lord, when He was betrayed, endured it with all patience; He did not strive, He did not cry out, nor in the streets did any one hear Him crying out. (Matthew 12:19) Therefore do ye also keep silence, quietness, and peace; and hinder not my martyrdom, but rather get yourselves also ready beforehand as athletes to the Lord, in order that you may overcome threatenings by a soul that has no fear of man, and that you may get the better of injuries through the endurance of the body. For this temporary fall is not to be feared; but that should be feared which has no end. The fear of men, then, is like smoke which, while it is raised and gathered together, disappears. And those torments ought to be feared which never have an end. For these torments, which happen to be somewhat light, any one can bear; but if they are heavy, they soon destroy life. But those torments are everlasting, where there are daily weepings, and mournings, and lamentations, and never-ending torture, to which the proconsul Ægeates is not afraid to go. Be therefore rather prepared for this, that through temporary afflictions ye may attain to everlasting rest, and may flourish for ever, and reign with Christ. (2 Corinthians 4:17)

The holy Apostle Andrew having admonished the people with these and such like words through the whole night, when the light of day dawned, Ægeates having sent for him, ordered the blessed Andrew to be brought to him; and having sat down upon the tribunal, he said: I have thought that you, by your reflection during the night, hast turned away your thoughts from folly, and given up your commendation of Christ that you might be able to be with us, and not throw away the pleasures of life; for it is folly to come for any purpose to the suffering of the cross, and to give oneself up to most shameful punishments and burnings.

The holy Andrew answered: I shall be able to have joy with you, if you will believe in Christ, and throw away the worship of idols; for Christ has sent me to this province, in which I have acquired for Christ a people not the smallest.

Ægeates said: For this reason I compel you to make a libation, that these people who have been deceived by you may forsake the vanity of your teaching, and may themselves offer grateful libations to the gods; for not even one city has remained in Achaia in which their temples have not been forsaken and deserted. And now, through you, let them be again restored to the worship of the images, in order that the gods also, who have been enraged against you, being pleased by this, may bring it about that you may return to their friendship and ours. But if not, you await varied tortures, on account of the vengeance of the gods; and after these, fastened to the tree of the cross which you commend, you shall die.

The holy Andrew said: Listen, O son of death and chaff made ready for eternal burnings, (Matthew 3:12) to me, the servant of God and apostle of Jesus Christ. Until now I have conversed with you kindly about the perfection of the faith, in order that you, receiving the exposition of the truth, being made perfect as its vindicator, might despise vain idols, and worship God, who is in the heavens; but since you remain in the same shamelessness at last, and think me to be afraid because of your threats, bring against me whatever may seem to you greater in the way of tortures. For the more shall I be well pleasing to my King, the more I shall endure in tortures for the confession of His name.

Then the proconsul Ægeates, being enraged, ordered the apostle of Christ to be afflicted by tortures. Being stretched out, therefore, by seven times three soldiers, and beaten with violence, he was lifted up and brought before the impious Ægeates. And he spoke to him thus: Listen to me, Andrew, and withdraw your thoughts from the outpouring of your blood; but if you will not hearken to me, I shall cause you to perish on the tree of the cross.

The holy Andrew said: I am a slave of the cross of Christ, and I ought rather to pray to attain to the trophy of the cross than to be afraid; but for you is laid up eternal torment, which, however, you may escape after you have tested my endurance, if you will believe in my Christ. For I am afflicted about your destruction, and I am not disturbed about my own suffering. For my suffering takes up a space of one day, or two at most; but your torment for endless ages shall never come to a close. Wherefore henceforward cease from adding to your miseries, and lighting up everlasting fire for yourself.

Ægeates then being enraged, ordered the blessed Andrew to be fastened to the cross. And he having left them all, goes up to the cross, and says to it with a clear voice: Rejoice, O cross, which has been consecrated by the body of Christ, and adorned by His limbs as if with pearls. Assuredly before my Lord went up on you, you had much earthly fear; but now invested with heavenly longing, you are fitted up according to my prayer. For I know, from those who believe, how many graces you have in Him, how many gifts prepared beforehand. Free from care, then, and with joy, I come to you, that you also exulting may receive me, the disciple of Him that was hanged upon you; because you have been always faithful to me, and I have desired to embrace you. O good cross, which hast received comeliness and beauty from the limbs of the Lord; O much longed for, and earnestly desired, and fervently sought after, and already prepared beforehand for my soul longing for you, take me away from men, and restore me to my Master, in order that through you He may accept me who through you has redeemed me.

And having thus spoken, the blessed Andrew, standing on the ground, and looking earnestly upon the cross, stripped himself and gave his clothes to the executioners, having urged the brethren that the executioners should come and do what had been commanded them; for they were standing at some distance. And they having come up, lifted him on the cross; and having stretched his body across with ropes, they only bound his feet, but did not sever his joints, having received this order from the proconsul: for he wished him to be in distress while hanging, and in the night-time, as he was suspended, to be eaten up alive by dogs.

And a great multitude of the brethren stood by, nearly twenty thousand; and having beheld the executioners standing off, and that they had done to the blessed one nothing of what those who were hanged up suffer, they thought that they would again hear something from him; for assuredly, as he was hanging, he moved his head smiling. And Stratocles inquired of him: Why are you smiling, Andrew, servant of God? Your laughter makes us mourn and weep, because we are deprived of you. And the blessed Andrew answered him: Shall I not laugh at all, my son

Stratocles, at the empty stratagem of Ægeates, through which he thinks to take vengeance upon us? We have nothing to do with him and his plans. He cannot hear; for if he could, he would be aware, having learned it by experience, that a man of Jesus is unpunished.

And having thus spoken, he discoursed to them all in common, for the people ran together enraged at the unjust judgment of Ægeates: You men standing by me, and women, and children, and elders, bond and free, and as many as will hear; I beseech you, forsake all this life, you who have for my sake assembled here; and hasten to take upon you my life, which leads to heavenly things, and once for all despise all temporary things, confirming the purposes of those who believe in Christ. And he exhorted them all, teaching that the sufferings of this transitory life are not worthy to be compared with the future recompense of the eternal life.

And the multitude hearing what was said by him, did not stand off from the place, and the blessed Andrew continued the rather to say to them more than he had spoken. And so much was said by him, that a space of three days and nights was taken up, and no one was tired and went away from him. And when also on the fourth day they beheld his nobleness, and the unweariedness of his intellect, and the multitude of his words, and the serviceableness of his exhortations, and the steadfastness of his soul, and the sobriety of his spirit, and the fixedness of his mind, and the perfection of his reason, they were enraged against Ægeates; and all with one accord hastened to the tribunal, and cried out against Ægeates, who was sitting, saying: What is your judgment, O proconsul? You have judged wickedly; your awards are impious. In what has the man done wrong; what evil has he done? The city has been put in an uproar; you grieve us all; do not betray Cæsar's city. Grant willingly to the Achaians a just man; grant willingly to us a God-fearing man; do not put to death a godly man. Four days he has been hanging, and is alive; having eaten nothing, he has filled us all. Take down the man from the cross, and we shall all seek after wisdom; release the man, and to all Achaia will mercy be shown. It is not necessary that he should suffer this, because, though hanging, he does not cease proclaiming the truth.

And when the proconsul refused to listen to them, at first indeed signing with his hand to the crowd to take themselves off, they began to be emboldened against him, being in number about twenty thousand. And the proconsul having beheld that they had somehow become maddened, afraid that something frightful would befall him, rose up from the tribunal and went away with them, having promised to set free the blessed Andrew. And some went on before to tell the apostle the cause for which they came to the place.

While all the crowd, therefore, was exulting that the blessed Andrew was going to be set free, the proconsul having come up, and all the brethren rejoicing along with Maximilla, the blessed Andrew, having heard this, said to the brethren standing by: What is it necessary for me to say to him, when I am departing to the Lord, that will I also say. For what reason have you again come to us, Ægeates? On what account do you, being a stranger to us, come to us? What will you again dare to do, what to contrive? Tell us. Have you come to release us, as having changed your mind? I would not agree with you that you had really changed your mind. Nor would I believe you, saying that you are my friend. Do you, O proconsul, release him that has been bound? By no means. For I have One with whom I shall be for ever; I have One with whom I shall live to countless ages. To Him I go; to Him I hasten, who also having made you known to me, has said to me, Let not that fearful man terrify you; do not think that he will lay hold of you, who art mine: for he is your enemy. Therefore, having known you through him who has turned towards me, I am delivered from you. But if you wish to believe in Christ, there will be opened up for time, as I promised you, a way of access; but if you have come only to release me, I shall not be able after this to be brought down from this cross alive in the body. For I and my kinsmen depart to our own, allowing you to be what you are, and what you do not know about yourself. For already I see my King, already I worship Him, already I stand before Him, where the fellowship of the angels is, where He reigns the only emperor, where there is light without night, where the flowers never fade, where trouble is never known, nor the name of grief heard, where there are cheerfulness and exultation that have no end. O blessed cross! Without the longing for you, no one enters into that place. But I am distressed, Ægeates, about your own miseries, because eternal perdition is ready to receive you. Run then, for your own sake, O pitiable one, while yet you can, lest perchance you should wish then when you can not.

When, therefore, he attempted to come near the tree of the cross, so as to release the blessed Andrew, with all the city applauding him, the holy Andrew said with a loud voice: Do not suffer Andrew, bound upon Your tree, to be released, O Lord; do not give me who am in Your mystery to the shameless devil. O Jesus Christ, let not Your adversary release me, who have been hanged by Your favour; O Father, let this insignificant man no longer humble him who has known Your greatness. The executioners, therefore, putting out their hands, were not able at all to touch him. Others, then, and others endeavoured to release him, and no one at all was able to come near him; for their arms were benumbed.

Then the blessed Andrew, having adjured the people, said: I entreat you earnestly, brethren, that I may first make one prayer to my Lord. So then set about releasing me. All the people therefore kept quiet because of the adjuration. Then the blessed Andrew, with a loud cry, said: Do not permit, O Lord, Your servant at this time to be removed from You; for it is time that my body be committed to the earth, and You shall order me to come to You. You who gives eternal life, my Teacher whom I have loved, whom on this cross I confess, whom I know, whom I possess, receive me, O Lord; and as I have confessed You and obeyed You, so now in this word hearken to me; and, before my body come down from the cross, receive me to Yourself, that through my departure there may be access to You of many of my kindred, finding rest for themselves in Your majesty.

When, therefore, he had said this, he became in the sight of all glad and exulting; for an exceeding splendour like lightning coming forth out of heaven shone down upon him, and so encircled him, that in consequence of such brightness mortal eyes could not look upon him at all. And the dazzling light remained about the space of half an hour. And when he had thus spoken and glorified the Lord still more, the light withdrew itself, and he gave up the ghost, and along with the brightness itself he departed to the Lord in giving Him thanks.

And after the decease of the most blessed Andrew the apostle, Maximilla being the most powerful of the notable women, and continuing among those who had come, as soon as she learned that the apostle had departed to the Lord, came up and turned her attention to the cross, along with Stratocles, taking no heed at all of those standing by, and with reverence took down the body of the most blessed apostle from the cross. And when it was evening, bestowing upon him the necessary care, she prepared the body for burial with costly spices, and laid it in her own tomb. For she had been parted from Ægeates on account of his brutal disposition and lawless conduct, having chosen for herself a holy and quiet life; and having been united to the love of Christ, she spent her life blessedly along with the brethren.

Ægeates had been very importunate with her, and promised that he would make her mistress of his wealth; but not having been able to persuade her, he was greatly enraged, and was determined to make a public charge against all the people, and to send to Cæsar an accusation against both Maximilla and all the people. And while he was arranging these things in the presence of his officers, at the dead of night he rose up, and unseen by all his people, having been tormented by the devil, he fell down from a great height, and rolling into the midst of the market-place of the city, breathed his last.

And this was reported to his brother Stratocles; and he sent his servants, having told them that they should bury him among those who had died a violent death. But he sought nothing of his substance, saying: Let not my Lord Jesus Christ, in whom I have believed, suffer me to touch anything whatever of the goods of my brother, that the condemnation of him who dared to cut off the apostle of the Lord may not disgrace me.

These things were done in the province of Achaia, in the city of Patras on the day before the kalends of December, where his good deeds are kept in mind even to this day, to the glory and praise of our Lord Jesus Christ, to whom be glory for ever and ever. Amen.

www.ingramcontent.com/pod-product-compliance
Lightning Source LLC
LaVergne TN
LVHW091320080426
835510LV00007B/580